W9-AIL-775

I Loved Jesus *in the* Night

I Loved Jesus *in the* Night

Teresa of Calcutta

A SECRET REVEALED

PAUL MURRAY

PARACLETE PRESS
BREWSTER, MASSACHUSETTS

I Loved Jesus in the Night: Teresa of Calcutta—A Secret Revealed

2008 First Printing

ISBN: 978–1–55725–604–1

This edition published by Paraclete Press, 2008.
First published in Great Britain by
Darton, Longman and Todd Ltd
1 Spencer Court
140–142 Wandsworth High Street
London SW18 4JJ

Designed and produced by Sandie Boccacci
Set in 12/14.25pt Centaur
Printed and bound in Great Britain

10 9 8 7 6 5 4 3 2 1

Published by Paraclete Press
Brewster, Massachusetts
www.paracletepress.com

To be in love & yet not to love,
to live by faith and yet not to believe.
To spend myself
and yet to be in total darkness.

Teresa of Calcutta

Mother Teresa's sandals

CONTENTS

FOREWORD

Mother Teresa died in 1997. Since that time, in slow and gradual leaks, astonishing evidence has emerged concerning her long dark night. This evidence (her 'deepest secret' as she called it), now that it has been fully revealed, has been for many people the cause of considerable shock and bewilderment. Questions unthinkable even a few years ago have begun to be raised, and not only by the secular media but also by a number of concerned believers. Is it possible, they ask, that Mother Teresa was somehow deceiving the world for years, feeling compelled to hide the truth of her distress? Or was she simply suffering from a form of depression? Or did she, in fact, actually lose her faith in the end?

When, a number of years ago, I first began this work, my intention, apart from noting down a few personal recollections of Mother Teresa, was to offer a brief reflection on the mystery and meaning of the 'darkness' which she endured for so many years. That still remains my intention. But now, in the light of all the bewilderment and confusion which has arisen of late, I have an added hope: namely, that this small book might serve as the beginning of an answer to some of the most recent and most urgent questions concerning Mother Teresa's dark night.

I am well aware, of course, that there are many other people whose knowledge of Mother Teresa is far more extensive and more profound than my own. Nevertheless, with the conviction that any kind of direct, personal knowledge of a great saint – however modest or limited that knowledge might be – is of manifest value, I have thought it worthwhile here to include, in these pages, a brief record of my meetings with 'the saint of Calcutta'. My principal aim in doing this is so that those among my contemporaries who find themselves drawn to the figure of Mother Teresa, but who never had the opportunity of meeting her when she was alive, by reading over the few small stories and anecdotes contained in this book, will be able to encounter her, for the space of an hour, perhaps, not as an abstract figure of holiness from the past – a revered figure in stone – but as I knew her: a living woman, a living saint.

ACKNOWLEDGEMENTS

The text of the present work was, for the most part, completed more than three years ago. My debt of gratitude, therefore, extends back in time to those generous friends who were among the first to encourage me in the task, and also to those few who, with scrupulous care and attention, read over some of the early drafts. I am especially grateful to Fr Jeremy Driscoll, O.S.B., Mary Redmond, and Fr Philip McShane, O.P. Thanks are also due to a number of the Sisters of Mother Teresa, the Missionaries of Charity, who were generous in sharing with me something of their first-hand knowledge of the saint, and also to two outstanding priests who knew her well over a number of years, William G. Curlin, the Emeritus Bishop of the Diocese of Charlotte, North Carolina, and Fr Josef Neuner, S.J., who was one of the early spiritual directors of Mother Teresa. To Fr Brian Kolodiejchuk, M.C., and to the Mother Teresa Centre, I owe a unique debt of gratitude for permission to quote extensively from the writings of

Mother Teresa. Apart from a number of comments or observations which I heard directly from Mother Teresa, and which it is a pleasure to record, the voice heard for the most part, in these pages, comes from the 'private writings' of the saint. Other people to whom I am indebted for their encouragement include Ed Martin, Susan Portieri, Fr Luke Dempsey, Fr Jim Quigley, Fr Michael Champagne, Joan Greatrex and Sr Kathy Wolff.

I am particularly grateful to Declan Murray of MC Design for his help with the design of the cover. The photographer responsible for most of the images on the inside pages of the book is an old acquaintance of Mother Teresa, Ciro Casella. My heartfelt thanks to him. Finally, I have to confess that in spite of every effort to discover the photographer responsible for the wonderful image of Mother Teresa reproduced on the front cover, the publisher has been unable to do so. Please write to my friends at Darton, Longman and Todd in London if you can help us properly credit this beautiful picture in future editions of this book.

Photograph by John McColgan

Mother Teresa and Paul Murray, 2 August 1991

I

A Teaching about Hunger

I HAD MY FIRST GLIMPSE OF Mother Teresa more than thirty years ago. The place where we met was an unexpected place: not in the streets of Calcutta among the poorest of the poor, not in a hospice for the dying, or in an orphanage for small children, but in a normal-sized university classroom in Rome. Like almost everyone else in the world, at that time, I had heard stories about her great goodness and love for the poor. But nothing could have prepared me for the impact she made on me at that first encounter. She spoke for just over thirty minutes, beginning her talk with a prayer and ending with a prayer. Together with my fellow students, I had listened, over the months, to many words being spoken in that particular classroom. But I had never realised that words of such simplicity and candour could so deeply penetrate the mind and heart.

It is almost impossible to describe the quality of Mother Teresa's voice. Her words, when she spoke, were not the expression of thoughts merely, or even of convictions, but somehow the expression of her entire being. She spoke slowly, her voice grave for the most part, and yet never mournful. Once or twice she repeated a sentence or two from the New Testament, but her first words were about hunger: 'Jesus has made the hunger of the poor His hunger and their thirst His thirst. He is that close to us. Will we turn away?' Then she quoted from the First Letter of St John: 'How can you say you love God whom you cannot see if you do not love your neighbour whom you can see?' She spoke, for a few moments, of the extent of suffering in the world and of the great hardship which the poor have to endure. But she went on, at once, to say that perhaps the greatest hunger in the world, the most terrible anguish, was not physical poverty or deprivation. It was the anguish of not being wanted, of being forgotten or rejected, of having no one.

Three years later, on 10 June 1977, I met Mother Teresa again, in Cambridge, England, and this time I was able to speak with her for a few moments alone. What struck me at once was something which has been remarked on many times over the years by those fortunate enough to meet Mother Teresa, and that is the radiant joy which shone in her face, a joy which, from moment to moment, seemed to illumine her every expression. At the time I wondered if I had ever, in my whole life, met anyone so radiant.

2

The Radiance, the Darkness

Mother Teresa died on 5 September 1997. Since then new information has begun to surface concerning the details of her own interior life. And this information has surprised and even shocked many of those who lived close to her for years, and thought they knew her well. For it now emerges that, in marked contrast to the shining, external radiance of Mother's presence among us, her *inner* world (the unseen, hidden places of her mind and heart) were, for many years, and to her own great bewilderment, caverns of a seeming emptiness, zones of an almost total darkness. No wonder she could exclaim in a letter written once to a priest: 'If I ever become a saint – I will surely be one of "darkness".'[1] This darkness was not, as will soon become clear in the pages which follow, an experience of depression or despair. Rather it was the shadow cast in her soul by the overwhelming light of God's presence: God utterly present and yet utterly hidden. His intimate, purifying love experienced as a devastating absence and even, on occasion, as a complete abandonment.

3

'God Wants to Use Nothing'

SINCE MOTHER TERESA'S DEATH IN 1997, apart from the revelations concerning the 'dark night' which she endured for so long, one other remarkable secret has come to light, a secret which, with characteristic modesty, she tried for years to keep hidden. It now appears that, as well as being a woman of enormous practical kindness, Mother Teresa was also the recipient of a series of mystical visions and locutions. She experienced these graces immediately, or almost immediately, before beginning her work in the slums for the poorest of the poor. Jesus was asking her directly, and in a most vivid way, to change her life utterly, and asking her also to establish a new religious Society or Community of Nuns: 'I want Indian Nuns, Missionaries of Charity, who would be My fire of love amongst the poor, the sick, the dying and the little children.'[1] At that time (the year was 1946), Mother Teresa wrote: 'In all my prayers and Holy Communions He is continually asking, "Wilt thou refuse … ?"'[2] Alarmed at the thought of what was being asked of her, and conscious of her own littleness and weakness, Mother Teresa replied: 'My own Jesus – what You ask is beyond me – I can hardly understand half of the things you want – I am unworthy – I am sinful – I am weak.'[3] But, by way of response to these words, at some point later in the interchange between them, she hears Jesus saying to her: 'You are I know the most incapable person – weak and sinful but just because you are that – I want to use you for My glory. Wilt thou refuse?'[4] And again: 'Fear not. It is I who am asking you to do this for Me. Fear not. Even if the whole world is against you, laughs at you, your companions and Superiors look down on you, fear not – it is I in you, with you, for you.'[5]

The fact of being chosen for this particular work, in this particular way, was a matter of continual astonishment to Mother Teresa. I remember her remarking on three or four occasions: 'In this age, more than in any other, God wants to use *nothing*!' 'Nothing' I discovered, as time passed, was a word she liked to use a lot. On another occasion she declared: 'Father Paul, when you discover you're *nothing*, rejoice!' Here, as much as the accent of joy, the note of liberation is telling. For what Mother Teresa means by 'being nothing' is in no way connected to the cold imprisonment of self-mistrust, or to what is called nowadays 'low self-esteem'. It is true Mother Teresa always approached God in deep poverty of spirit. But, at the same time, with an equal profundity of spirit, she trusted absolutely in his love for her. Yes, there were trials she had to undergo, and there was darkness to be endured; and, yes, at times she made mistakes.[6] But, for all that, she was his 'little one', his spouse, his beloved. At the close of a strikingly beautiful meditation, composed when she was seriously ill in hospital in June 1983, she wrote: 'Jesus, I love with my whole heart, with my whole being. I have given Him all, even my sins, and He has espoused me to Himself in tenderness and love.'[7]

4

A Meeting in Rome

In early August 1991, I had occasion to go to Rome for just over a week, and it was suggested to me, by one of the Missionaries of Charity that I should go to meet Mother at San Gregorio, one of their convents in Rome. I was frankly hesitant about the idea, not wanting to waste her time. But when I finally phoned the convent, Mother Teresa herself came to the telephone, and at once warmly invited me to come the next day, the second of August, at 4.30 p.m.

Our meeting took place in the convent itself – a very poor convent by any standards. We sat down on the long, grey stone step which runs from one end of the building to the other. After a few minutes of conversation, I remarked to Mother Teresa that I had brought her a present. 'A present!' she exclaimed with manifest surprise. I then produced a card from under my habit, and gave it to her. On the back of the card, the evening before, I had written down a number of short statements or prayers attributed to St Bernadette Soubirous of Lourdes. The text itself was called *The Testament of St Bernadette.*[1] Child-like in spirit, it evokes in a most moving and vivid manner some of the minor and major moments of suffering – the 'dark nights' – endured by Bernadette at different stages during her life.

What inspired me to show this particular text, or parts of it, to Mother Teresa I can't imagine. I don't think that it ever occurred to me that Mother's experience would in any significant way correspond to that of the French saint, or that she might herself be undergoing the same anguish of the dark night. The small *Testament,* although concerned throughout with suffering and darkness, takes the form – astonishingly – of a prayer of gratitude and thanksgiving, a prayer which is addressed at times to Jesus and at times to Mary. Here are a number of extracts taken from the *Testament,* including a few which I wrote down on the card I gave to Mother:

> For the humiliation I received, for the mockeries, for the insults, for those who thought I was mad, for those who thought I was a liar, for those who thought I was self-

serving, thank you, Madonna.

Thank you, thank you, for if there had been on earth a child more ignorant and more stupid, you would have chosen her.

For my mother, dead and far away; for the affliction I suffered when my father, instead of opening out his arms to his own small Bernadette, called me 'Sister Marie-Bernard', thank you, Jesus.

Thank you for being Bernadette, threatened with prison because I had seen you, Holy Virgin; stared at by people as if I were a rare beast; that Bernadette so miserable that when people saw me, they said: 'Not this one surely?'

For this pitiful body that you have given me, this sickness of fire and smoke, for my decomposing flesh, for my decaying bones, for my sweats, for my fevers, for my hidden and intense anguish, thank you, O my God.

For this soul that you have given me, for the desert of interior aridity, for your nights, for your flashes of lightning, for your silences, for your thunder-strokes, for everything, for you, absent or present, thank you, Jesus.

Given the reality of Mother Teresa's own secret, interior affliction, the phrase 'hidden and intense anguish' would certainly have spoken directly to her heart. But she might also have identified with the humiliation endured by Bernadette.[2] Years later, when I was giving a retreat to the Missionaries of Charity in Calcutta, Mother Teresa said to me one day: 'Father Paul, it is possible that God may have given me the gift of humility. But, if he has, when I look back on my life, I realise that this gift was always accompanied by humiliation.' Then, she added, with a smile: 'Of course, they are not the same thing!'

I find it remarkable to note here that almost all the experiences of anguish, evoked in the *Testament*, find an echo in Mother Teresa's own earlier history. The *Testament* speaks, for example, of 'mockeries' and 'insults', and of the humiliation of being considered 'mad' by other people. Likewise, in the case of Mother Teresa, it soon became obvious that her new God-given task or mission would not be understood by the Congregation to which she belonged, the Loreto Sisters. She wrote in 1947: 'From my Superiors down, I know they will laugh at me. They will think me a fool, proud, mad etc.'[3] Again, worthy of note here is a comment made by Mother Teresa, on another occasion when, with the same astonished humility as the saint of the *Testament*, she expressed enormous surprise at being chosen by heaven for such an important mission: 'If He [God] could find a poorer woman through whom to do this work, He would not choose me, but He would choose that woman.'[4]

At one point, the *Testament* speaks of Bernadette's anguish at having to live her life as a religious, separated forever from her beloved parent: 'my mother, dead and far away'.[5] Also, as it happens, Mother Teresa suffered deeply, over many years, the fact of being separated from her mother. Owing to the difficult political situation in Communist Albania, mother and daughter were unable, in fact, to communicate for eleven long years. But, finally, in 1957, Mother Teresa was able to write: 'I had a long letter from my old mother. At last they received news of me ... In 1948 she heard I was leaving Loreto – & then nothing – so she thought I was dead.'[6] Again, the *Testament* speaks of Bernadette's experience of 'being stared at by people as if I were a rare beast'. In Mother Teresa's case, the fact that, for years, she was the object of fascinated and insistent attention by the world's media was an affliction she found particularly difficult to bear. Referring, for example, to one occasion in Philadelphia, when she was surrounded on all sides by milling crowds of people and by police, she describes the occasion as nothing less than a Station of the Cross.[7]

That said, the particular part of the *Testament* with which, I suspect, Mother Teresa most immediately identified was the very last sentence, the part which speaks directly of interior aridity and darkness. When I handed her the card, she began to read it slowly out loud. But her pace, I noticed, got slower and slower towards the end. She was clearly not just saying the words but praying the words. Her voice, when she began to read the last sentence in particular, was quieter than before, and she pronounced the words very distinctly and very slowly indeed. Then, when it was over, without another word, she closed her eyes and bent down her head. It was obvious she was praying. I waited. Moments passed. Finally, she lifted her head, and for a second I caught an expression in her eyes I find impossible to describe. Then, a moment later, with deep feeling, she said: 'But … *how* He speaks to us!'

In retrospect now, in view of the recent revelations concerning the mysterious dark night of spirit endured by Mother Teresa over so many years, it gives me no small joy to think that maybe by simply reading the *Testament,* that day in August 1991, the darkness surrounding her spirit may have lifted for a moment, or rather (I should say) for a moment revealed itself to her for what it really was, namely the intimate hidden radiance of God's presence.

5

A Saint of Darkness

NOT PERHAPS SURPRISINGLY Mother Teresa revealed to very few people the extent of the darkness she was enduring. But, in the earlier part of her life, she did entrust this knowledge to a few Jesuit Fathers in India who were, for a period, her spiritual directors and also, at one point, to Archbishop Ferdinand Périer of Calcutta. Here are some extracts from what might perhaps deservedly be called 'the letters of darkness':

> There is so much contradiction in my soul. – Such deep longing for God – so deep that is painful – a suffering continual – and yet not wanted by God – repulsed – empty – no faith – no love – no zeal … Heaven means nothing – to me it looks like an empty place … yet this torturing longing for God.
>
> (28 February 1957)[1]

> People say they are drawn closer to God – seeing my strong faith. – Is this not deceiving people? Every time I have wanted to tell the truth that – 'I have no faith' – the words just do not come – my mouth remains closed. – And yet I still keep on smiling at God and all. (21 September 1962)[2]

> In my soul – I can't tell you – how dark it is, how painful, how terrible … I feel like 'refusing God' and yet, the biggest and the hardest thing to bear is this terrible longing for God – Pray for me that I may not turn a Judas to Jesus in this painful darkness.
>
> (9 January 1964)[3]

> To be in love & yet not to love, to live by faith and yet not to believe. To spend myself and yet to be in total darkness. (17 May 1964)[4]

To anyone who imagines that the path of holiness is a path covered end to end with the roses of consolation these few extracts will serve as an immediate and sharp corrective. But why, it needs to be asked, if God was indeed so intimately present to Mother Teresa, why did she feel so abandoned? Why the 'torturing pain'? And if, in private, she was continually experiencing interior darkness and emptiness, how was it that she was able, in public, to live and proclaim what she believed with such manifest certitude?

6

The Meaning of the Dark Night

To BEGIN TO ATTEMPT AN ANSWER to these questions is almost a presumption in itself. For, obviously, no mere intellectual understanding alone can hope to grasp or interpret a mystery of such depth and magnitude. I am reminded here of a statement which was made once by the great Spanish mystic, St John of the Cross. Writing, in a different context, about other mysterious 'words and revelations' he noted that 'they embody an abyss and depth of spiritual significance, and to want to limit them to our interpretation ... is like wanting to grasp a handful of air.'[1] That said, some interpretation is needed. And, for guidance in this matter – given my own lack of experience – I can think of no one better to rely on than the Spanish Carmelite himself, St John of the Cross. Mother Teresa was familiar with the work of St John. Writing, on one occasion, to the Jesuit, Father Neuner, she remarked:

> [Y]ou will I am sure be surprised that the works of St John of the Cross seem to be books I am able to understand a little & enjoy sometimes. – His writings make me hunger for God – and then faced by that terrible feeling of being 'unwanted' by Him.[2]

John of the Cross is universally acknowledged (at least within the Western mystical tradition) as the most outstanding authority on the experience of the dark night. For John 'night' entails a radical purification of the soul's deep-rooted hurts and imperfections. It is, in fact, nothing other than an inner journey towards God, a wondrous hidden path of illumination. But so stark, at times, are John's descriptions of this '*noche oscura*' it is possible to forget that what is being described is, at root, an unimaginable blessing, an illumination so profound that it overwhelms all our faculties. In one simple phrase, John says it all: 'This dark night is an inflow of God into the soul.'[3] But this 'inflow' since it begins at once to effect a radical purification and transformation in the soul, is almost unbearable. That is why John speaks of it as 'this tempestuous and frightful night'.[4] He says: 'Both the sense and the spirit, as though under a dark load, undergo such agony and pain that the soul would consider death a relief.'[5] What is more, St John notes that, at this stage, the contemplative soul, feeling so completely wretched, begins even to imagine that God is *against* him or her.[6] No wonder, then, that in the midst of this 'dark night' Teresa of Calcutta – with the voice of someone abandoned – could cry out to God:

> In the darkness … Lord, my God, who am I that You should forsake me? The child of Your love – and now become as the most hated one – the one You have thrown away as unwanted – unloved. I call, I cling, I want – and there is no One to answer … The loneliness of the heart that wants love is unbearable … I have no faith. – I dare not utter the words & thoughts that crowd in my heart – & make me suffer untold agony … If there be God, please forgive me … When I try to raise my thoughts to Heaven – there is such convicting emptiness that those very thoughts return like sharp knives and hurt my very soul. – Love – the word – it brings nothing. – I am told God loves me – and yet the reality of darkness and coldness and emptiness is so great that nothing touches my soul.[7]

These strange and terrible words remind us that it is one thing to learn about '*la noche oscura*' intellectually; it is quite another thing to experience it. We may be informed reassuringly, by the mystical tradition, that the dark night is nothing other than the in-pouring of God's light into the soul – a grace of unimaginable depth and wonder – but those who experience this night undergo such suffering and such loneliness, they begin (St John of the Cross explains) to believe 'there will be no more spiritual blessings for them, and that God has abandoned them'.[8] John writes: '[W]hat the sorrowing soul feels most is the conviction that God has rejected it, and with an abhorrence of it cast it into darkness. The thought that God has abandoned it is a piteous and heavy affliction for the soul ... [it] feels very vividly indeed the shadow of death, the sighs of death, and the sorrows of hell, all of which reflect the feeling of God's absence, of being chastised and rejected by Him.'[9] St John's language and imagery, at this point, are so extreme one might be inclined to think that the experience described is one peculiar to himself. But, in a private note, composed in the form of a prayer in 1959, Mother Teresa writes: 'They say people in hell suffer eternal pain because of the loss of God ... In my soul I feel just that terrible pain of loss – of God not wanting me – of God not being

God – of God not really existing.'[10]

At times, so overwhelmingly oppressive is the experience of the dark night, it can easily be confused with a state of depression, or with what St John of the Cross calls 'melancholic humour'.[11] For that reason John, in his work, is at pains to underline the difference between a person suffering from depression and someone undergoing the 'dark night'. The depressed individual, John explains, lives in a state of continual self-preoccupation, whereas the contemplative's whole concern and anxiety, during the time of darkness and aridity, is with being unable *apparently* to give whole-hearted service and attention to God. Again and again, therefore, no matter how bewildering the experience of the dark night, the contemplative, John says, turns to God with a sustained, inward solicitude and with anxious care.[12]

7

Varieties of the Dark Night

WHAT DREW COUNTLESS NUMBERS of people to love and admire Mother Teresa, over many years, was the manifest joy which shone in her every gesture. But, in the light of the new revelations concerning her 'darkness', I think it is probably true to say that we find ourselves closer to her now than ever before, and in a way which is totally new and unexpected. In particular, with regard to those among us who feel bewildered, at times, or even completely lost, but who are determined to keep walking along the path of faith, Teresa of Calcutta has become a source of enormous encouragement, a truly remarkable example of steadfastness and hope.

That said, it is important to note here that not every experience of 'darkness' in prayer should be interpreted as a sign of mystical grace. To begin to think along those lines would be not only dangerous but silly. If, for example, someone has not yet been able to get free from the bondage of sin or from addiction, then, at the time of prayer or meditation, it is almost inevitable that he or she will experience some cloud of sadness in their spirit, some shadow of darkness. This does not mean, of course, that because they are sinners, or because they are weak, God will refuse to listen to their prayer. On the contrary. The 'darkness' they experience is merely a sign of guilt or shame or need. But it is not a sign that God is somehow against them or that, for any reason, God will refuse to come near them when they call. In fact, the very opposite is the case. But neither does this 'darkness' indicate, as I have said, the beginnings of the mystical life and the mysterious onset, therefore, of the 'dark night'. For that to be the case, certain other signs must be present, and all of these, needless to say, we can see manifest in the prayer experience of Mother Teresa.

According to St John of the Cross, there are three signs which mark the beginning of the dark night, understood in the strict sense of the word:[1] first, the person seeking God begins to lose the original delight and satisfaction he or she used to have in the things of God and in the things of the world. Prayer itself, as a result, loses all its savour; it becomes unutterably dull and bone-dry. Second, the person begins to suspect they are now turning back instead of going forward. They continue to pray, of course, and continue to show the same loving respect for their neighbour. But, at the same time, they are plagued by the thought that somehow they have lost their way in the spiritual life, and are no longer serving God. Third, and last, in their practice of meditation, they find they are simply unable to return to their original way of prayer, in which there was not only great consolation but also a role for the senses and the imagination, and in which it was possible for the mind, without too much effort, to reflect on the things of God in a discursive manner.

At this point, according to St John of the Cross, God begins to communicate Himself 'through pure spirit by an act of simple contemplation, in which there is no discursive succession of thought'.[2] It is a movement towards a much deeper intimacy, a much deeper prayer. But, for the faculties of sense and spirit and imagination which are unable, because of natural limitation, to attain to this mystery, it is inevitably a dark night. John of the Cross notes further that this state or stage of contemplation, although in itself a momentous blessing, is for the most part 'secret and hidden from the very one who receives it'.[3] And that was certainly the case with Mother Teresa.

It should be obvious, by now, that the writings of John of the Cross offer a number of useful, interpretive keys for understanding the puzzle and mystery of Mother Teresa's 'dark night'. Nevertheless, between these two saints – these two 'authors' – there is one thing that is noticeably different. John of the Cross, being not only a poet but also a scholastic theologian, is never shy to use, in his work, technical terms such as 'active night of the senses' and 'passive night of the spirit'. In contrast, Teresa of Calcutta instinctively avoids all these terms. Both in her talks and in her writings, whether by instinct or design, she prefers to keep close to the simple language of the Gospel.

The risk in evoking the categories of traditional mysticism in order to come to some understanding of the 'darkness' endured by Mother Teresa is that the great simplicity of her life will somehow be obscured. But, of course, there is nothing whatever esoteric about this tiny saint. Her experience of the dark night does, it is true, draw our attention towards the unspeakable mystery of God. But her compelling description of the night of faith also draws us into the very heart of human anguish and human longing. Something which Pope John Paul II said, on one occasion, about the writings of John of the Cross, can be said here, and with at least equal validity, about the letters of darkness of Mother Teresa. John Paul remarked first on the fact that, in the writings of John, the dark night appears 'as a typically human and Christian experience'.[4] To anyone familiar with the literature of mystical theology, this statement is an unexpected one. In what sense can the dark night of someone like John of the Cross be described as 'typically human'? Where is the connection between the night of faith of the Christian mystic and our common human suffering? John Paul explains:

> Our era has lived through dramatic moments: the silence or absence of God; the experience of disasters and suffering such as wars or even the holocaust of so many innocent people. All such moments have led to a better understanding of this expression of his ['the dark night'] giving it the character of a collective experience, applicable to the very reality of life and not just to a stage along a spiritual path.[5]

This means that men and women, in modern times, undergoing the pain of their own profound anguish, might well be able to find, in the contemplative 'nights' of John and Teresa, an unexpected witness to hope. Speaking, in that vein, concerning the impact of the Spanish mystic on the contemporary world, John Paul does not hesitate to extend the meaning of the night of faith to embrace some of the most terrible forms of human suffering in our time. He writes:

> The Saint's teaching is invoked today in the face of the immeasurable mystery of human suffering ... Physical, moral or spiritual suffering, such as illness, the scourge of hunger, war, injustice, loneliness, the meaninglessness of life, the very fragility of human existence, the sad awareness of sin, the apparent absence of God: for the believer all of these are a purifying experience which might go under the name of the night of faith.[6]

8

The Feelings of an Unbeliever

THOSE WHO HAD THE PRIVILEGE OF meeting Mother Teresa during her life, or of hearing her speak, knew they were in the presence of a woman who possessed great certitude with regard to matters of faith. How, then, are we to explain those writings of Teresa of Calcutta which, at times, seem to suggest profound doubt about God's very existence? One pointer towards an understanding, I would suggest, is a comment John of the Cross makes in *The Ascent of Mount Carmel,* in which he highlights the dual and paradoxical nature of faith. He writes: 'though faith brings certitude to the intellect, it does not produce clarity, but only darkness'.[1] This darkness is a trial for every believer. For, in spite of the certitude which faith brings, the act of faith itself is always opaque and resistant to reason. It is a radical, affirmative assent to truth, but it is not a direct *seeing.*

Its assent, no matter how confident and sustained, is always obscure. And this fact inevitably awakens in the believer a certain 'mental unrest'.[2] Even the 'ordinary' believer can *feel*, at times, like an unbeliever. And this *feeling* often develops into a profound anguish as soon as the darkness of the night of faith begins to deepen.

The feeling of 'being unwanted' by God, of being somehow rejected by God, is an experience which has been described in the past, and over and over again, by Christian saints and mystics. But, writing in 1923, the Benedictine Dom John Chapman observed that 'the *corresponding trial* of our contemporaries seems to be the *feeling of not having any faith;* not temptations against any particular article (usually), but a mere feeling that religion is not true'.[3] Well, it may indeed be the case that the phenomenon described here by Chapman has greatly intensified in our own age. Nevertheless, that phenomenon itself – the sudden, sinking feeling of having lost all faith in God and in religion – is, in fact, a trial which has afflicted many Christian believers in the past. It is obviously not something restricted, therefore, to people of unusual intellectual or spiritual gifts. Countless numbers of men and women who have kept faith, over the years, with the practice of prayer, but who regard themselves as ordinary and unremarkable, have on occasion lost all sense of the presence of God during the hours of prayer. They might not wish to identify, perhaps, with the full meaning of the words of Blessed Johannes Tauler, the medieval Dominican mystic and preacher, when he describes the dark night of faith, but they would certainly understand him when he declares: 'then we are so abandoned that we have no further knowledge of God, and we come into such distress that we do not know if we have ever been on the right path, we do not know whether God exists or not.'[4]

Even in the most profound night of faith, the terrible *feeling* of no longer being capable of believing in God, although a cause of the most profound anguish, does not represent for the individual believer a loss of faith, or even what is sometimes referred to nowadays as 'a crisis of faith'. On the contrary, it is a stage of radical purification, a graced bewilderment, a rite of passage towards an even deeper communion with God.

9

'Where is Jesus?'

In the case of Mother Teresa, it was not simply the darkness weighing on her inner heart which constituted the anguish of the night. What most troubled her spirit was what she called 'this torturing longing for God'.[1] Thus, on 6 November 1958, she wrote: 'I did not know that love could make one suffer so much. – That was suffering of loss – this is of longing – of pain human but caused by the divine.'[2] In this state, John of the Cross explains, the soul lives by one thing only: namely, the 'driving force of a fathomless desire for union with God'.[3] And, as a result, 'the absences of the Beloved which the soul suffers … are very painful; some are of such a kind that there is no suffering comparable to them.'[4]

One spiritual friend or confidant with whom over a number of years Mother Teresa shared something of her experience of the dark night was an

American priest called William Curlin. He was invited in January 1983 to give a retreat at the Mother House in Calcutta. At that time he was pastor in a parish in Washington D.C. A number of years later he was ordained bishop, and is now Bishop Emeritus of the Diocese of Charlotte, North Carolina. During the retreat Father Curlin found himself speaking one evening with Mother Teresa on the subject of 'spiritual aridity'.[5] A sister who was nearby, overhearing their conversation and convinced, no doubt, that such aridity or such interior darkness could never have been the ordinary experience of Mother Teresa, remarked: 'Mother must have had great consolation from God to support her mission to the poorest of the poor'! Given what we know now about the devastating lack of consolation endured by Mother Teresa over so many years, this statement, for all its simplicity, must have had quite a strong and immediate impact. According to Bishop Curlin, Mother Teresa, clearly unwilling to be drawn into a conversation which would focus attention on the issue of her own interior darkness, slipped quietly away.[6]

That evening, however, during the Holy Hour when Father Curlin, in company with a number of the Sisters, was praying in silent adoration before the Blessed Sacrament, one of the sisters delivered into his hand a note written moments before by Mother herself. It contained a message both brief and stark: 'Father, please pray for me. Where is Jesus?' Father Curlin immediately glanced over at Mother Teresa, and she returned his gaze. But, then, she went down on her knees at once and, lifting her joined hands in prayer, turned her gaze back to the Blessed Sacrament exposed on the altar.

Father, please
pray for me –
Where is Jesus?

Photo of handwritten note passed to Father Curlin

The pain – the unrelenting pain – occasioned by 'the absence' of her Beloved marked the spiritual experience of Mother Teresa for the rest of her life. And yet, during all those years, she somehow found courage to surrender to God's will, and to keep on surrendering. On one occasion she wrote: '[T]he darkness is so dark, and the pain is so painful. – But I accept whatever He gives and I give whatever He takes.'[7] As much as any of her acts of kindness or charity, it was that capacity to surrender, that desire to be faithful and to hold fast, day after day, year after year, in blind and trusting faith, which marked the holiness of Mother Teresa. No doubt we will continue to regard her, and for good reason, as a woman of indomitable will and conviction. But, glimpsed now in the light of the new revelations concerning her inner darkness, she is revealed as belonging – if not at the deepest level of spirit then at the most immediate level of feeling – to the poorest of the poor, an icon for all those who live bewildered lives, a saint of the wounded and the broken-hearted.

One of the very few people with whom she spoke openly about her experience of the dark night, was a Jesuit priest in India called Father Josef Neuner. I was privileged, just before I finished the present work, to receive a letter from Father Neuner (at the time he was 97 years old) in which he spoke of Mother's 'prolonged dark night'. In his letter he remarked: 'Most people know nothing of it – she remains the ideal of compassionate love only – they do not see the spiritual basis of her spirituality. Jesus has saved us by being with us in our condition and darkness, living it in communion with His Father, an unbroken communion with us in our broken world . . . This is the core of her charism.'[8]

10

Absence and Presence

MOTHER TERESA, SPEAKING IN A noticeably weak voice on the telephone to her friend, Bishop Curlin, not long before she died, remarked: 'My key to heaven is that I loved Jesus in the night.'[1] But even for her – for this tiny, devoted 'saint of darkness' – there was to be a brief opening of the clouds, a period of respite. Once, during a Mass celebrated in the Cathedral in Calcutta, having prayed for some sign or 'proof' that God was pleased with the Society she had founded, the Missionaries of Charity, she experienced a quite extraordinary illumination. 'There & then,' she writes, 'disappeared that long darkness, that pain of loss – of loneliness – of that strange suffering of ten years.' And she adds: 'Today my soul is filled with love, with joy untold – with an unbroken union of love.'[2]

Like all contemplatives of the mystery of God,

Mother Teresa chooses, at times, to speak of the experience of prayer in very simple, positive terms. But, at other times, she reveals how prayer can be accompanied by a terrible sense of emptiness. Prayer in itself, however, she insists, is not meant to be a continual torment. Yes, there are times of enormous difficulty and even of heart-break in prayer, and times of such utter dullness of spirit it seems we are simply unable to pray. So what, then, are we to do? What are we to think? In a talk which she gave on 8 January 1980, Mother Teresa addressed this question with directness and simplicity. Her words which, at one point, refer to those dark hours when it seems indeed we are incapable of prayer, are words full of encouragement. She writes:

> [P]rayer is not meant to be a torture, not meant to make us feel uneasy, is not meant to trouble us. It is something to look forward to, to talk to my Father, to talk to Jesus, the one to whom I belong: body, soul, mind, heart. And when times come when we can't pray, it is very simple: if Jesus is in my heart let him pray, let me allow Him to pray in me, to talk to His Father in the silence of my heart. Since I cannot speak – He will speak; since I cannot pray – He will pray. That's

> why often we should say: 'Jesus in my heart, I believe in your faithful love for me.'[3]

There were many hundreds of letters written by Teresa of Calcutta during her lifetime – thousands of pages. But, on the subject of prayer, there is one brief statement, in one of the letters, I find particularly moving. It is a comment which betrays a depth of spiritual intimacy, a hidden supernatural love, for which there are almost no words. She writes:

> My love for Jesus keeps growing more simple and more, I think, personal ... I want Him to be at ease with me – not to mind my feelings – as long as He feels alright – not to mind even the darkness that surrounds Him in me – but that in spite of everything Jesus is all to me and that I love no one but only Jesus.[4]

What is noteworthy about this passage, and there are many comparable passages in the 'private writings' of Mother Teresa, is that, in spite of being profoundly disturbed by the 'darkness' surrounding her at this time, the bewildered 'saint of darkness' does not turn in on herself like a melancholic, or like someone suffering from depression. Instead, her whole preoccupation is with caring for her Beloved, concentrating first and last on *his* comfort not her own, turning to her hidden Master and Lord with a quite remarkable tenderness; and, in spite of the devastating trial of darkness and aridity, behaving towards God, as St John of the Cross once expressed it, 'solicitously and with painful care'.[5]

II

Christian Faith and the Dark Night

It might be wise, at this point, to pause for a moment and note once again the puzzlement expressed by one of Mother Teresa's sisters in Calcutta regarding the 'absence' of God during the dark night. To this good woman it seemed inconceivable that someone living and working like Mother Teresa would be asked to endure the torment of spiritual aridity and darkness. 'Mother,' she declared, 'must have had great consolation from God in order to support her mission to the poorest of the poor.' The statement certainly sounds like basic common sense. But, in fact, it is now generally accepted that saintly and courageous men and women quite often lived and worked for years without any notable consolation of spirit. Accordingly, the long trial of 'darkness' endured by Mother Teresa should not, it would seem, be regarded as something entirely out of the ordinary. Nevertheless, a considerable number of people – readers of this text among them – will still, I suspect, find themselves identifying with the robust immediacy and directness of the sister's earlier comment. For so overwhelming, at times, is the anguish endured by Mother Teresa, during her long 'dark night', it compels us to confront a number of sharp and difficult questions.

To begin with, does the simple following of the Gospel path really require such a frightening depth of spiritual and emotional distress? Is the Father of Christ Jesus not revealed to us in the New Testament as a God of love 'in whom there is no darkness at all?' (1 John 1:5). How, then, are we to understand the connection between Mother Teresa's experience of the dark night and the illumined faith of the ordinary believer? Has the Christian faith-experience not been linked, over the centuries, with a certain interior sense or felt awareness of God's presence? And has this saving grace of awareness not been attested to, again and again, by many of the greatest and most revered Christian saints and mystics? These questions touch on matters which are at the very core of the Christian faith. Obviously, it would be foolish to imagine that a satisfactory answer could be given here within the space of a few paragraphs. Nevertheless, I think some kind of answer should be attempted.

First of all, it is clear that very few Christian believers are asked to undergo the depth of spiritual anguish experienced by Mother Teresa during the dark night. This holds true even for the members of the religious congregations and institutes inspired or directly founded by Mother Teresa. Some years ago, Cardinal Ratzinger (the present Pope Benedict XVI) made an interesting observation regarding the dark night of St John of the Cross. What he said on that occasion can, I think, be applied today with equal force and relevance to the dark night of Teresa of Calcutta. Ratzinger wrote: 'The "dark night" described by St John of the Cross is a part of his personal charism of prayer. Not every member of his Order needs to experience it in the same way so as to reach that perfection of prayer to which God has called him.'[1] Clearly wanting to give special emphasis to this point, Ratzinger noted further: 'There are certain mystical graces conferred on the founders of ecclesial institutes … which characterise their personal experience of prayer and which cannot, as such, be the object of imitation and aspiration for other members of the faithful, even those who belong to the same institutes.'[2]

At a depth almost unimaginable to the ordinary believer, Teresa of Calcutta handed herself over entirely to Christ, allowing Him to live – or *re-live* –

his passion, death and resurrection within her. But this grace of illumined faith, this paradoxical experience of an almost total spiritual darkness, although different in *degree* – vastly different – from the faith-experience of the ordinary believer, is not different in *kind*. Christian faith, while it involves (even for the least believer among us) a clear and saving knowledge of God, is in itself also a kind of darkness. We know this, and perhaps most keenly of all, in the experience of prayer. It is not at all necessary, therefore, to be a great mystic or a profound contemplative in order to identify – at least at some level – with the following short statement about prayer from a celebrated medieval text:

> In the beginning it is usual to feel nothing but a kind of darkness about your mind ... You will seem to know nothing and to feel nothing except a naked intent toward God in the depth of your being ... You will feel frustrated, for your mind will be unable to grasp him, and your heart will not relish the delight of his love. But learn to be at home in this darkness. Return to it as often as you can, letting your spirit cry out to him whom you love.[3]

The frustration referred to here and the 'darkness' can, at times, make 'ordinary' believers begin to panic, and imagine they are perhaps losing their faith. But this is not at all the case. And, in fact, during this time of trial, believers will often find great encouragement in the witness and courage of those contemplatives who, over the centuries, dared to keep faith with God even when, at times, the 'darkness' they were experiencing must often have felt like the darkness of atheism. An illuminating reflection on this subject can be found in an open letter composed by a group of contemplative monks in 1967 and sent to all the Bishops who, that year, were gathering in Rome for a special Synod. In the letter, we read:

> Drawn into the spiritual desert by his own vocation, the contemplative ... knows all the bitterness and anguish of the dark night ... But he also knows, through the life of Christ, that God is victor over death ... Familiar with a God who is 'absent' and as though 'non-existent', as far as nature is concerned, the contemplative ... understands how the temptation of atheism which assails some Christians can, in the last analysis, strengthen their faith in a testing which is not without analogy to the 'nights' of the mystics.[4]

What follows, then, is a passage of such faith conviction and of such impressive force and beauty it is, I am persuaded, well worth quoting here in full:

> The desert lays bare our heart; it sweeps away our pretexts, our alibis, our imperfect images of God; it reduces us to the essential; it places us before our own truth, leaving no possibility of escape. This can be beneficial to faith itself. For it is then, at the very heart of our misery, that the marvels of God's mercy are manifested. At the heart of our 'gravity' is 'grace', the extraordinary power of God 'which is effective only in our weakness' ... Though it traverses desert paths – which may resemble those over which the temptation to atheism can lead – the experience of the contemplative is not negative. The absence of the transcendent God is also, paradoxically, His immanent presence.[5]

Why the experience of faith is, at its core, so utterly mysterious and not a simple matter of clear and distinct ideas, is because the object of faith – the *primary* object – is not a clear-cut series of dogmas to which we give our intellectual assent. That would reduce faith to a mere ideology. No – by faith we attain to something far more wonderful. With the hand of faith we reach out and actually touch, as it were, and at a level of intimate communion, the Word who is Life. This 'contact' is sometimes experienced in the form of a vivid felt perception when for an hour, perhaps, or for a few moments only, we experience a profound sense of the presence of God. But more often, in practice, even when the 'contact' is most real, there is no felt perception of any kind. And that is what is meant by the dark night.

12

Paradox or Contradiction?

'PEOPLE SAY THEY ARE DRAWN CLOSER to God – seeing my strong faith. – Is this not deceiving people?'[1] More than once, in her private writings, Mother Teresa put this question to herself, and with manifest bewilderment. The root cause of her bewilderment was the marked contrast between, on the one hand, the fountain or river of blessing which seemed to pour out, through her, to others from God and, on the other hand, the utter coldness, darkness, and aridity of her own interior spirit. On one occasion, to a particular friend, she confessed: 'when I open my mouth to speak to the sisters and to people about God and God's work, it brings them light, joy and courage. But I get nothing out of it. Inside it is all dark and feeling that I am totally cut off from God.'[2] It would appear then that, with regard to the question of her darkness, Mother

Teresa herself remained confused for many years. On 8 November 1961 she wrote: 'I don't know what is really happening to me.'[3] And again, earlier in the same year: 'My very life seems so contradictory.'[4] No wonder she could, on one occasion, find herself praying: 'Jesus, don't let my soul be deceived – nor let me deceive anyone.'[5]

Given the reality of her own interior anguish, it clearly took a huge effort on the part of Mother Teresa to keep her hope and her courage alive every day, and to keep smiling. But what a devastating experience to have to bear, day after day, the apparent split or contradiction between her smiling exterior self on the one hand and, on the other, her inner heart's deep unhappiness. Was there, as some commentators have recently suggested, so utter and complete a split here between image and reality, that her life in the end, in spite of its acknowledged virtue and sheer goodness, assumed almost the form of a deception, a kind of hypocrisy? Was the joy which, on the outside, brought manifest blessing and encouragement to so many people across the world, a false joy, a forced joy? Or was there, in spite of the darkness and coldness *within*, something of light and warmth there also, a hidden joy, a fire of love unseen, unfelt – even by Mother Teresa herself – an emotion not of the heart but of the spirit, and yet something so strong and so alive, it found expression, and over and over again, in the simple, unaffected radiance and warmth and joy of Mother Teresa's presence? I have no doubt whatever that the latter hypothesis is the correct one. But if that is indeed the case how, it needs to be asked, is it possible for two opposite conditions of soul, namely great affliction and great joy, to be present together *simultaneously* in someone like Teresa of Calcutta?

One of the most helpful answers to this question has been given by Pope Paul VI. He points out that the Christian believer can, in fact, 'have two hearts: one natural, the other supernatural'.[6] Accordingly, very different things such as affliction and joy 'are not only possible together,' he writes, 'but compatible'.[7] And he says further: 'the Christian can at one and the same time have two different, opposite experiences which become complementary: sorrow and joy'.[8] Thus we can say that, with her natural heart, or at the level of ordinary feeling, Mother Teresa experienced utter and complete desolation. But, at a much deeper level (at that level where supernatural grace is most at work), she was aware of being intimately united with the will of God. '[T]here is in my heart,' she writes, 'a very deep union with the will of God. I accept not in my feelings – but with my will.'[9]

Well worth noting, in this context, is a short passage from a Christmas letter Mother Teresa wrote in 1959. In it we can see, and with wonderful clarity, the three separate dimensions of Mother Teresa's experience: first, the simple delight she takes in the joy of others around her; second, her heart-rending awareness of the terrible darkness and loneliness within; and, third, her astonishing joy at being one with the will of God. She writes:

> Thank God all went well yesterday, sisters, children, the lepers, the sick and our poor families have all been so happy and contented this year. A real Christmas. – Yet within me – nothing but darkness, conflict, loneliness so terrible. I am perfectly happy to be like this to the end of life.[10]

13

The Sunshine of Darkness

Mother Teresa did, as we know, continue to suffer intensely her dark night until the very end. But her attitude to the experience underwent, in time, a significant change. Gradually, she came to regard the darkness not only as a share in Christ's passion but also, in some sense, as 'the spiritual side of her apostolate.' She wrote: 'I have come to love the darkness – For I believe now that it is a part, a very, very small part of Jesus' darkness & pain on earth.'[1] And to her friend, Bishop William, at their last meeting in 1995, she remarked, and repeated several times: 'What a wonderful gift from God to be able to offer Him the emptiness I feel. I am so happy to give Him this gift.'[2]

For Mother Teresa the gift was 'wonderful,' first of all because it underlined her intimate communion with God. But also because she realised that her experience of the dark night, her feeling of being unloved and unwanted, could help in some way to unite her more closely with the poorest of the poor. She wrote: 'Let Him do with me whatever He wants … If my darkness is light to some soul … I am perfectly happy.'[3] And again: 'The physical situation of my poor left in the streets unwanted, unloved, unclaimed – are the true picture of my own spiritual life.'[4]

In the summer of 1960 Mother Teresa made another striking reference to her experience of the dark night. It is a matter of only a few words, a tiny phrase. Nevertheless, in its use of the language of paradox, the statement might almost have come from the pen of G. K. Chesterton. Halfway through a letter to a friend, all of a sudden, with an unexpected, pithy directness, Mother Teresa exclaimed: 'With me the sunshine of darkness is bright.'[5] The statement certainly sounds positive. But, considering the period at which it was written, it would seem likely that what Mother Teresa intended to communicate here (although not without a saving touch of irony) was that her 'darkness' was, in fact, just as intense and dark as ever. Significantly and movingly, the next sentence reads: 'Pray for me.' Nevertheless, whether or not she intended to place emphasis here on spiritual anguish or on spiritual joy, the phrase itself, when looked at in the light of Mother Teresa's *later* understanding of her 'darkness', certainly seems to call for a distinctly positive reading, an acknowledgment, in other words, that the terrible darkness she endured for so long – that long night which seemed so empty of love and empty of meaning – was, at its deepest core, nothing less, in fact, than the mysterious and brilliant light – the paradoxical *sunshine* – of God's presence.

We are often inclined to forget that Teresa of Calcutta, as well as being an 'icon of holiness' for people all over the world, was also a woman of flesh and blood. Speaking about herself, on one occasion, she remarked: 'By nature I am sensitive, [I] love beautiful and nice things, comfort and all that comfort can bring – to be loved and love.'[6] How much it must have cost her, therefore, to endure that long dark night of feeling so unloved and unwanted. But what a relief, finally, to begin to realise that it was precisely because of the darkness of her dark night that she was able, in the end, to carry something of the light of Christ into the 'dark holes of the slums'.[7] In her life of prayer, in her inner life, God appeared, for years, to be so completely remote it was as if he had abandoned her. Nevertheless, without the least hesitation she was able to assert, and with simple gratitude: '[W]hen I walk through the slums or enter the dark holes – there Our Lord is always really present.'[8]

14

The Gift of 'Nothing'

DAY AFTER DAY, HOUR AFTER HOUR, in very humble meetings – one to one – with the lonely and the poor, with the sick and the abused, with the most abandoned, it was there, in those encounters, that Mother Teresa recognised most of all the 'thirst' of God. This fact explains, I think, the great care and reverence she showed to those in any kind of distress. She approached the poor, in fact, with almost the same humility with which she approached God. On one occasion, at the *Casilina* Convent in Rome, she said to me: 'The poor don't need our compassion, Father Paul, they need our help. We need their compassion.'

In the August of 1991, I was invited by Mother Teresa to visit her at the Convent of San Gregorio in Rome. When I arrived there, however, I found the place filled with journalists. Apparently, Mother

Teresa had declined to do an interview, but the journalists refused to go away. The interview, they told her, would be reproduced across the world; it would be written up in all the major journals. They were simply helping her, they said, to get her message across to the world. Mother Teresa still refused, saying gently 'Not today, thank you.' When, finally, they left, taking with them all their lights and cameras and equipment, Mother Teresa and I sat down. We began to talk. Almost the first thing she said was: 'You know, they don't understand. Jesus came into the world with the most important message of all time, and he had only thirty-three short years to communicate it. And he spent thirty years doing *nothing!*'

On another occasion, again using the word 'nothing' to no small effect, Mother Teresa said to me: 'If, Father Paul, at the time of prayer or meditation it seems to you that not only have you been distracted in your prayer, but that you have done nothing at all, never leave that time or that place of prayer angry or bitter with yourself. First – turn to God and give God that *nothing!*' There, in that last tiny phrase, is revealed not only something of the spiritual genius of Mother Teresa, but also something of the utterly mysterious humility of God. I remember, on another occasion, in the midst of a conversation in the Mother House in Calcutta, she exclaimed all of a sudden: 'That God is high, transcendent, all-powerful, almighty, I can understand that because I am so small. But that God has become small, and that he thirsts for my love, *begs* for it – I *cannot* understand it, I *cannot* understand it, I *cannot* understand it!'

Sister Nirmala, Mother and Father Paul at their last meeting, 24 May 1997.

15

Mother Teresa at Mass

It was always, I felt, a great privilege to be able to pray with Mother Teresa, whether simply saying the rosary with her and her sisters on occasion or else celebrating Mass. On the last occasion we met, 24 May 1997, about three months before her death, I was invited to be the celebrant at an early Mass in the chapel at Casilina, the largest of the sisters' houses in Rome. It was the day when a number of young sisters would take solemn vows at a special public Mass. But Mother Teresa decided that there should also be a 'private' Mass earlier in the day for the Missionaries of Charity themselves. It was a celebration of great peace and great joy. The small chapel in Casilina was packed with members from some of the different branches of the Missionaries of Charity, both active and contemplative. All of us, I think, in the chapel that day were aware of our great privilege. There are moments, in all our lives, of extraordinary grace and blessing. That hour at Casilina was for myself a 'moment' of that kind, one I will never forget. As it turned out, it was to be the last Mass I would ever celebrate with Mother Teresa.

The daily ritual of the Mass – the 'breaking of the bread' – for all its unmatched mystery and beauty, was never for Mother Teresa a practice of religion in any way separate from the task of working for the poorest of the poor. On the contrary. 'In the Mass,' she would say, 'we have Jesus in the appearance of bread, while in the slums I see Christ in the distressing disguise of the poor. The Eucharist and the poor are but one love for me.'[1] And again: 'The Mass is the spiritual food that sustains me. I could not pass a single day or hour in my life without it.'[2]

The humble manner in which Mother Teresa assisted at Mass every day betrayed – it often seemed to me – almost a desperate need to be fed by the Bread of Life. It is true she would kneel with great stillness before the altar and with utter simplicity. But there were times in the Mass when she would suddenly lift her eyes up to the altar, looking almost like a beggar in need, so raw it seemed, and so profound, was her hunger for God. Even during the preaching of the homily, I remember, there was no one in the entire chapel who would look so poor and needy in spirit, so hungry to receive the Word of Life. Nothing, I think, in a priest's or a preacher's life could be more humbling than that.

16

A Mission to Love

Mother Teresa always signed 'MC' after her name. She was first and last a Missionary of Charity – and a very practical one at that. Her focus was on the world outside herself, and on those most in need of help and attention. In this book I have already quoted a number of things which she said and wrote, things which reveal in part the secret of her own interior life. But, except to a very small number of people, Mother Teresa never spoke of these things. She never tried to draw attention to herself. Even when she was suffering some acute physical pain, she would try to hide her distress, and focus her attention on the people around her.

One instance comes to mind. Early in May 1993, she fell and broke three ribs. The doctors wanted to keep her in hospital but she very quickly discharged herself. I met her shortly afterwards at Casilina, where I'd been invited one morning to celebrate Mass for her and the sisters. At the Mass that morning there was another priest who concelebrated, an American I'd never met before. The sisters prepared a simple breakfast for us afterwards, and while we were eating, Mother Teresa came to greet us. She was her usual welcoming self – smiling and, it seemed, relaxed. But I noticed that, in spite of the brave front, there was great pain showing in her eyes. As so often, when she spoke in those years, her conversation turned to the subject of China, and to her great longing to be able to send, as soon as it became possible, missionaries to China. The priest, who was there with us, asked: 'Mother Teresa, is there any particular group you're hoping to *target* in China?' The question was innocent enough, but the language used was, of course, that of international big business, *not* that of the Gospel. Mother Teresa showed not the least sign of displeasure. Instead, she replied simply and at once: 'My great desire is to meet anybody who has nobody.'

Mother Teresa's attention was directed, first and last, to the poorest of the poor throughout the world. But she found time also to meet with and encourage people of all types and classes. It was part of her mission of charity. One letter which she wrote to Malcolm Muggeridge, and which may well have helped him towards his eventual conversion, reveals not only her simplicity of heart and strength of faith but also the depth and passion of her mind. Here is an extract:

> I think I understand you better now. – I am afraid I could not answer to your deep suffering … I don't know why, but you are to me like Nicodemus (who came to Jesus under cover of night), & I'm sure the answer is the same – 'Unless you become a little child …' I am sure you will understand beautifully everything – if you would only 'become' a little child in God's hands. Your longing for God is so deep, and yet He keeps Himself away from you. – He must be forcing Himself to do so – because He loves you so much – as to give Jesus to die for you & for me. – Christ is longing to be your Food. Surrounded with fullness of living Food, you allow yourself to starve. – The personal love Christ has for you is infinite. – The small difficulty you have re[garding] His Church is finite. – Overcome the finite with the infinite. – Christ has created you because He wanted you. I know what you feel – terrible longing – with dark emptiness – &

yet He is the one in Love with you.[1]

There are several statements in this letter which are memorable, but the phrase or statement which has perhaps the most resonance, given all that we have learned recently about Mother Teresa's own inner darkness, is the statement: 'I know what you feel – terrible longing – with dark emptiness.' But, in the end, of course, the brief, final statement: 'and yet He is the one in love with you' is the statement of absolute and supreme importance. Not once but many times I heard Mother Teresa repeat this statement, now in one form, now in another. It is a message at the core of her mission: *He is the one in love with you.*

17

Mother Teresa and the Small Thérèse

TOWARDS THE END OF JANUARY 1995 I was in Calcutta in order to give some retreats and talks to the Missionaries of Charity. One morning, after celebrating Mass in the Mother House, Mother Teresa took time to serve my breakfast. We were sitting together in a small room near the Chapel, and present also was one of the MC brothers who had come to attend Mass that morning. Although Mother Teresa normally avoided speaking about herself, on this occasion she volunteered one small detail concerning her religious name 'Teresa'. This name is one which is traditionally associated with the great Spanish mystic, St Teresa of Avila. 'When I joined religious life,' Mother Teresa said, 'I was hoping to take the name Thérèse after St Thérèse of Lisieux, but there was already, at that time, a Sister called Thérèse in the community. I wanted the name of the *small* Teresa not the big Teresa!'

Before this conversation took place I had, for some years, been struck (as had others who had come to know Mother) by the manifest links between her spirituality and that of Thérèse. Accordingly, when in late May 1997, I was asked to preach at the Mass in Casilina with Mother Teresa present, I decided I would include in the homily an extract or two from the writings of the French saint. More than a full century earlier, on 2 August 1893, Thérèse had written a letter to Celine, her blood sister. It was a remarkable letter, and one which, in fact, Mother Teresa herself might well have written. In the letter Thérèse speaks, first of all, of the paradox of God's presence in our lives, a presence that feels like absence. She writes: 'He hides, is wrapped in darkness.'[1] But that darkness is nothing other than a mysterious illumination, the radiance of His presence. Thérèse explains: 'Jesus loves you with a love so great that if you saw it, you would be in an ecstasy of happiness of which you would die, but you do not see it and you suffer.'[2]

In my homily that morning I quoted a longer passage from the letter of Thérèse in which she quotes from St Matthew's Gospel the great, saving words which Jesus will proclaim on the last day. This particular text from the Gospel is one which Mother

Teresa had come to regard as of supreme importance for her own life and mission. Thérèse writes:

> He [Jesus] makes himself poor that we may be able to do him charity; he stretches out his hand to us like a beggar, that upon the sunlit day of judgment, when he appears in his glory, he may be able to utter and we to hear the loving words: 'Come, blessed of my Father; for I was hungry and you gave me to eat: I was thirsty and you gave me to drink: I was a stranger and you took me in; I was in prison, sick, and you came to me.' It was Jesus himself who uttered those words, it is he who wants our love, begs for it. He puts himself, so to say, at our mercy. And the smallest thing is precious in his divine eyes.[3]

In religious literature it is not uncommon to read descriptions of saints and sinners who asked for God's mercy, or who begged His help. What is remarkable about this passage from Thérèse is that the one begging and pleading is God himself. This thought, this vision, is something that was for Mother Teresa almost an obsession. She believed, and with an intense and living faith, that it was not only in the broken Host we see before us on the altar, but also in the person whom we see to be afflicted or in great need that Jesus *thirsts* for our love, begs for our attention. In early February 1994, when she spoke at the National Prayer Breakfast in Washington DC, Mother Teresa quoted the text from St Matthew's Gospel that Thérèse had included in her letter to Celine.[4] But, then, she went on at once to complete the quotation, drawing attention to one of her own favourite sayings in the Gospel: 'In so far as you did this [kindness] to one of these, the least of my brethren, you did it to me.'

Mother Teresa not only liked to repeat this quotation, she would also sometimes try to bring its message home with a small gesture at once serious and playful. Thus, on two occasions, I remember – once in Rome and once in Calcutta – she took my hand in her hand, and repeating the Gospel passage, spelt out the Gospel words on my five fingers: 'You-did-it-to-me'. Then she said: 'The entire mystery of our lives is here, Father Paul, in these five words.'

18

The Demands of Love

'ARE YOU MARRIED?' On one occasion this question was put to Mother Teresa in a manifestly playful spirit by an American professor. And, at once, Mother Teresa replied: 'Yes, and I sometimes find it very difficult to smile at my spouse, Jesus, because He can be very demanding.'[1] This reply, though just as playful in its tone as the question itself, draws attention to an aspect of the life and experience of Mother Teresa which is at the very core of her vocation. It is, I think, impossible, to exaggerate the demands made on her by her beloved 'spouse', and I have in mind here especially the very first months when she began her work in the slums of Calcutta. For, right from the beginning of her life as a Missionary of Charity, her will, it seemed, was being tested in a crucible of suffering. And the experience bewildered her. She began to feel on her shoulders, as it were – and as never before – the burden of the cross. On 16 February 1949, she wrote in a private notebook: 'Today I learned a good lesson – the poverty of the poor must be often so hard for them. When I went round looking for a home – I walked & walked till my legs & arms ached – I thought how they must also ache in body and soul looking for home – food – help.'[2] Then, a few lines later, she added: 'This is the dark night of the birth of the Society. – My God give me courage now – this moment – to persevere in following Your call.'[3]

The great trial for Mother Teresa, at this time, was not her life and work in the slums. That was certainly hard for her to bear. But what was immeasurably more difficult was the experience, in these weeks and months, of feeling suddenly and completely abandoned by God. It was no accident that, in the entry for 16 February, she instinctively used the phrase 'the dark night'. Just over a week later, on 28 February, she wrote: 'Today – my God – what tortures of loneliness. – I wonder how long my heart will suffer this . . . Tears rolled & rolled.'[4] The God of consolation, whom for months she had heard speaking in her inmost heart, and whom she had seen in mystical vision, was now silent. Instead of the immediacy of grace and consolation – the felt presence of Jesus, her spouse – there was nothing but darkness and emptiness. Clearly astonished by this phenomenon, she wrote: 'there is such terrible darkness within me, as if everything was dead. It has been like this more or less from the time I started "the work."'[5]

In time, Mother Teresa would come to understand this period of trial – this 'dark night' – as a sign of God's favour, a proof even that her total offering of self had been accepted. Thus, on 14 January 1969, she was able to write to a contemplative Dominican friend in the United States, Sister Mary of the Trinity: 'Darkness may cover your soul after the surrender but be happy that it is like that – for that too is the living proof that He has accepted you.'[6] This statement is one born of living faith, and it is remarkable. But it must never be forgotten that, to the most immediate understanding of the mind, and to the ordinary emotions of the heart, darkness still feels like darkness. In spite, therefore, of Mother Teresa's profound faith-understanding of the 'dark night' – her happy discovery that it is a sign and proof of God's love – this long night of interior darkness experienced month after month, year after year, and the tough, unrelenting pressure of the demands of love, must have been almost impossible to bear.

19

A Grace of Surrender

How Mother Teresa's 'yes' to God survived this trial over so many years is a mystery for which there are no words. For what we are privileged to glimpse here is an encounter between the infinite freedom of God and the finite freedom of an individual soul. Nevertheless, we cannot help but ask ourselves if there is any concept or any category which could begin to explain the readiness of someone like Teresa of Calcutta to do the whole of God's will no matter what the cost. Hans Urs von Balthasar, reflecting on this subject in one of his writings, speaks of 'an active-passive readiness to receive the *whole* Word.'[1] It is, he says, 'a burning readiness to be used and consumed for the salvation and redemption of the world ... a readiness that will necessarily be expressed as personal oblation, as the prayer of surrender.'[2]

Although, in this passage from Balthasar, we find no reference to the life or experience of Teresa of Calcutta, the passage could almost have been written with her particularly in mind. And that holds true also, I believe, for the following rather unexpected statement: 'Where this readiness is reached, God can, should he so choose, load onto a person more than he or she can humanly bear ... And this readiness to take on more than is humanly possible leads directly ... to the Christian passion.'[3] The fact that Mother Teresa kept saying 'yes' and allowed herself to be stretched far beyond what a person can humanly endure, helps to explain why, though consumed by the love of God, she would so often ask people to pray for her, and not only lay helpers, religious sisters and priests, but also the poorest of the poor whom she served.[4] In my own experience as a priest, I have to say that no one in my whole life ever asked me to pray for them so often, and with such insistence as Mother Teresa – a fact which astonishes me now when I think of it.

The one occasion which remains most vivid in my mind with respect to this matter, took place one afternoon in the summer of 1991 at the Convent of San Gregorio in Rome. Already, earlier that day, during a brief meeting in the sacristy after Mass, Mother Teresa had said to me: 'Pray for me, Father

Paul, that I won't spoil God's beautiful work.' Later, in the afternoon, when we met by chance in the open passage-way which forms the centre of the convent, she again asked for prayers. On this occasion she was standing on the long grey stone step, a position which enabled her to look directly into my eyes. Putting her two hands over my hands, as if to join them in prayer, she said: 'Please pray for me, Father Paul. I need your prayers much more than you need mine.' Then, she opened her hands, and opened her arms wide and, to my great astonishment, exclaimed: 'I am so exposed to the whole world!' As she did this, and as she spoke, I remember noticing that both her outstretched hands and arms were trembling.[5]

20

Profound Vision, Simple Words

THERE IS A STORY FROM THE early Desert Fathers about a certain Abba Lot who went to see the ancient monk and saint, Abba Joseph of Panephysis. Lot said to Abba Joseph: 'Abba, as far as I can I say my little office, I fast a little, I pray and meditate, I live in peace and as far as I can, I purify my thoughts. What else can I do?' Then, according to the ancient text, Abba Joseph, we are told, 'stood up and stretched his hands toward heaven. His fingers became like ten lamps of fire and he said to him, "if you will, you can become all flame."'[1] This remarkable story comes to mind when I think of Mother Teresa. For as I got to know her a little over the years, she impressed me as someone so completely caught or taken by the fire of God's love, she had indeed become a flame.[2] Again and again I noticed that what one might call this element of fire in her spirit, this radiance, shone in a particular way when she was speaking about God, or when she was in the presence of someone in need.

In this context I remember, in particular, one unforgettable conversation which took place in Rome. It was again the August of 1991. Mother Teresa, after our meeting on the grey stone step in San Gregorio, had asked me to come back, two weeks later, to give a retreat to the sisters. One day, during that retreat, I found myself alone with her for half an hour, sitting around a wooden table in the tiny sacristy of the convent. She spoke and I listened. And she spoke mostly of God, and of God's love. Her words, I remember, were utterly simple. There was nothing original in what she said, nothing at all to astonish or impress. But somehow between the words, or behind the words, I sensed an enormous depth – an ocean of awareness. At one point in the conversation, when she made what is, perhaps, the most basic statement anyone can make about God, it sounded on her lips almost like a revelation: 'Father Paul', she said, 'God is love!'

At certain times, during this particular conversation, Mother Teresa looked, I remember, more joyful than I'd ever seen her before. She continued to talk, and I continued to listen. But then something unusual happened – a moment of grace and blessing which took me completely by surprise. And it still amazes me now when I think of it. It concerned my mother. I had never, as it happened, even once, spoken of my mother to Mother Teresa. And that fact is one element in the surprise. My mother, a widow at that time, was living in Belfast in the North of Ireland. She had always been a devoted mother, and a woman of prayer. But soon after my father's death, several years earlier, she had suffered a nervous breakdown. Eventually, I am happy to say, she recovered. But then, to her own very considerable distress and ours (we were a family of eight children) she would begin, every so often, to dip back into the black depression. And this would happen maybe about once or twice a year.

Several months before the conversation took place with Mother Teresa in Rome, I had spent the Christmas holiday at home with my mother. It was a very difficult time, for she was again the victim of one of those sustained black moods. And, since all of us in the family loved her so much, we were naturally heart-broken. I began, from that time, to pray to Christ Jesus for my mother. I had prayed to God before, but never with such insistence and desperation. I remember, for example, saying to Christ in prayer, and with almost as much impatience, I suspect, as trust: 'Lord, you simply cannot let my mother spend her last years in this way!'

21

A Small Miracle?

EIGHT MONTHS LATER, sitting and talking with Mother Teresa in the sacristy of the convent at San Gregorio, I was not of course thinking about my mother. But concern for her must, I imagine, have been the unspoken prayer in my heart. I say this because of what happened next. Mother Teresa suddenly stopped speaking in mid-sentence. She looked at me as if she had seen in my eyes, or in my expression, something she had not noticed before. Then, to my astonishment, she stood up, and said: 'Excuse me, Father Paul. I'll be back!' In a second she was gone out the door. About six or seven minutes later she returned, carrying in her hand a small envelope. She gave it to me, and said: 'Please, Father Paul, give this to your mother'. Since the envelope was open, I looked inside it as soon as our conversation was over. And there, to my surprise, I found a short letter addressed to my mother. It began with the phrase, 'Dear Mother of Fr Paul Murray', and was signed at the bottom: 'M. Teresa MC.'

A few weeks later, when I brought the letter home to my mother, she was obviously delighted. I think she presumed I must have asked Mother Teresa to write to her. Needless to say, she regarded it as a great blessing simply to have received a letter, even a tiny one, from such a source. But the blessing, as it turned out, was greater than she could have guessed. For, in the years that followed – her last years – my mother never again fell back into the black depression for any significant period. Like all of us, of course, she had occasional swings and changes in mood. But thanks, I believe, to the wholly unexpected intervention of grace through Mother Teresa, she was at last free of the affliction which had dogged her for years.

I don't know if there are other instances of a similar kind in the life of Mother Teresa. What seems to have happened in this case – and here, of course, I can only guess at the workings of providence – is that, moved by Christ within her, Mother Teresa was able somehow, in that instant, to 'read my soul', and was prompted by God's grace to answer the need of my mother and the unspoken prayer of my heart. On more than one occasion, Mother

Teresa would speak of herself as a pencil in the hand of God – and no wonder! In this case, so swift was her response to grace, it seemed indeed as if another hand, another *mind,* had moved her to write the letter. In fact she moved, it seemed to me, almost before she had time to think. Needless to say, I have no words to express my sense of gratitude and wonder at this gift.

22

A Spirit of Freedom and Joy

ENDOWED WITH A GREAT DEAL of common sense, Mother Teresa was never staid or standoffish. She possessed, in fact, a very lively sense of humour, and few things pleased her so much as the exuberant joy she witnessed, again and again, in the young women who had come to join her Congregation to work for the poorest of the poor. Concerning one group of MC aspirants, for example, whom she had visited just before setting out on a train journey in 1966, she wrote: 'The Epiphany Aspirants – 34 – young, healthy, full of zeal – make the house vibrate with laughter. I have had little chance to enjoy their company – but I can hear them even in the train – as my heart and mind is [are] very close to them.'[1]

Over the years I noticed that Mother Teresa was always the first to catch a joke in a homily or to see the humour in any given situation. Writing to a friend, on one occasion, from whom, it would appear, she hoped to receive a letter – and *soon* – she made the following 'complaint': 'When I write regularly – the sisters say I am in the 1st class, if less 2nd and 3rd class. When I neglect them they say I am in Zero class. I think I will put you also in Zero class if you don't write'![12] Again, something of Mother Teresa's sharp wit and great good humour is apparent in a comment which she made during a talk delivered in 1981: '...once I was asked, "What will you do when you are not Mother General any more?" I said, "I am first class in cleaning toilets and drains."'![13]

The rule of life Mother Teresa followed – that of the Missionaries of Charity – determined almost everything she did, every day, down to the smallest detail. And yet she always seemed to breathe an air of freedom. She was a woman of joy. And that joy and that freedom were much in evidence when, on one occasion in Rome, she astonished a number of us with her spirit of playfulness and good humour. The occasion was the blessing of a dormitory space for some poor, elderly women whom the sisters housed and looked after in their convent, Dono di Maria, situated just inside the Vatican. Pope John Paul II had originally allotted space for a home and convent to be built there some years before. But, hearing that the women in the home needed even more space, Pope John Paul gave permission to the sisters to extend the women's dormitory right up to the walls of the papal audience hall. Present at the small ceremony of blessing were the women themselves, Mother Teresa, some of her sisters, some lay-helpers and a small scattering of priests. I was fortunate to be there myself since, at that time, I was the sisters' regular confessor.

The only other person present was a bishop who had come that day in order to perform the blessing. We stood around him in an open space (a sort of small yard of the convent) while he conducted the ceremony. He began first with a prayer, and then, before the actual blessing, he started to give a short homily. He spoke for a minute or two, I remember, of the great kindness of Pope John Paul who had originally taken the initiative in making land available, several years before, for the building of the home for the poor. We must, he said, be very grateful to the Pope: first, for that original generosity, but also for the new initiative he had taken in offering more space for the building of the dormitory. The bishop then remarked on the Pope's active, personal interest in the work of the sisters at Dono di Maria, and began once again to repeat his earlier words about being grateful to the Pope.

At this point there was, all of a sudden, an interruption from the front row. Mother Teresa spoke, and I thought I heard what she said. But I could scarcely believe it. Then, with a smile on her face, pointing her finger straight up into the air, she again repeated her original statement: 'We must thank the Lord first!' I imagine that the good bishop would have got around, in time, to saying something like that himself. But, in fact, up to this point in his homily, he had not yet mentioned God or Jesus Christ but had spoken only of the Pope. In the wake of Mother Teresa's intervention the bishop looked, understandably, a bit bewildered. But then, after a moment's hesitation, smiling a little to himself, he continued on with his homily. For her part, Mother Teresa – to my astonishment – continued to keep her index finger pointing straight up into the air. And, while she did this, she glanced over for a second to where I was standing, and in a voice, a half-whisper, at once serious and playful, she exclaimed, 'The *Lord!*' I was stunned for a moment. And, I have to say, it cost me no small effort to stop myself shaking with laughter. Finally, when at last Mother Teresa took down her finger – the homily of the good bishop having continued on, all this while, unabated – I noticed she was wearing a very impish grin on her face.

The moment passed. From one point of view, it

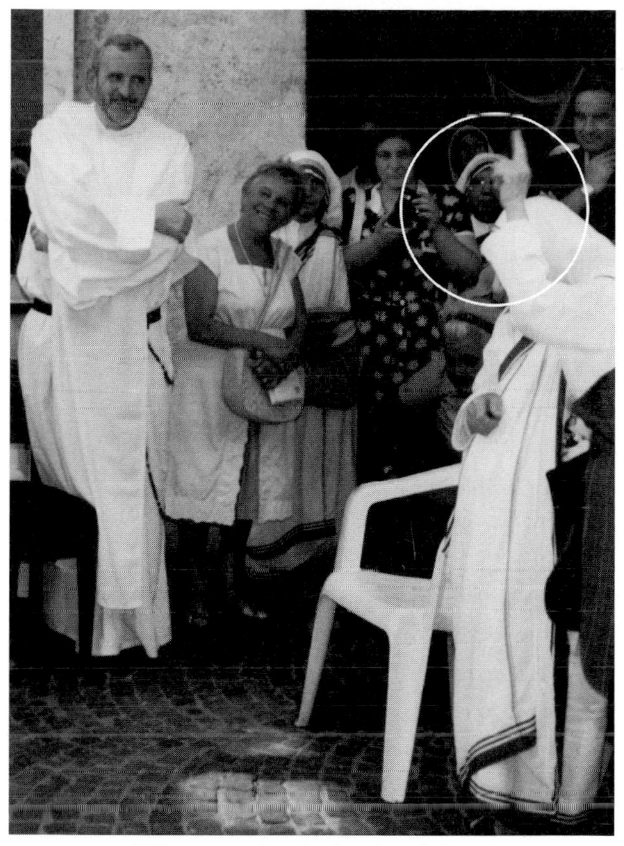

'We must thank the Lord first!'

was simply a burst of exuberance – a playful, unscripted gesture made possible by the intimacy of the gathering. But from another point of view it was,

I think, revelatory. For though carried off with a lightness of touch that hurt no one, the gesture – for those of us who saw it – brought home to us at once one of the great truths of our faith. We are all of us naturally grateful for the many different ministries of service within the Church, and that includes, of course, and in a most especial way, the Petrine or the Papal ministry. But this tiny, dramatic gesture of Mother Teresa served to remind us that our gratitude in life must go first and last to God, the author of all good gifts and blessings. No matter how privileged our role within the Church might be, at best we are but instruments of God's wonderful grace. It is, I believe, the particular task of the saint within the Church to remind us of this truth. And no one, I think, could have done it with a more child-like exuberance or with greater panache than Mother Teresa that day in the Vatican.

By chance someone with a camera who was present took a series of photos of the entire incident. But, even if there were no photos, the image of Mother Teresa smiling broadly and pointing her finger up into the air would remain with me always. That gesture *and* her words: 'We must thank the Lord first!'

23

On Earth and in Heaven

Many thousands of people thronged St Peter's Square on the day of Mother Teresa's beatification. They had come from all parts of the world, the young and the old of all nations, men and women whose lives had been touched, in one way or another, by the light of God's goodness shining through this tiny Albanian woman. Several years earlier, Mother Teresa had written in a letter to a priest: 'If I ever become a saint – I will surely be one of "darkness". I will continually be absent from heaven – to light the light of those in darkness on earth.'[1] That astonishing image of being a saint, and yet 'absent from heaven' brings back into my mind a story which Mother Teresa told me once in Rome. It was at the convent at Dono di Maria. Mother Teresa had come first to Confession in the small convent chapel. But, then, we had an opportunity afterwards to meet just outside the chapel sitting at a small table. The 'story' she told me was not really a story in any ordinary sense of the word. It was, in fact, the account of a dream which she had had many years before. As she was telling me the details of the dream, Mother Teresa didn't laugh outright at any stage, but there was, I noticed, laughter in her eyes from start to finish. Here is the dream as she told it:

> One night during the first months of my work in the slums of Calcutta, I had a dream – it was like a vision. All of a sudden I found myself at the gates of Paradise. And I was delighted – filled with joy. But just as I was about to walk in through the gates, St Peter came out and blocked my way. 'You can't come in here,' he said, 'There are no slums up here!' I was furious with Peter. And I said to him at once: 'Alright, I will go back. But I'm going to return here, Peter. And I'm going to fill this heaven of yours with all of my people from the slums!'

This meeting with Mother Teresa took place on 26 October 1994. One week earlier, on 19 October, I had been asked to say early Mass for Mother, and about six or seven other people, in the tiny chapel at

Dono di Maria. (I discovered afterwards that someone, standing just inside the door, had been allowed to video certain parts of the Mass.) As far as I can remember, it was the only time I ever saw Mother Teresa looking, or at least appearing to look, utterly desolate. That was on 19 October 1994. A mere nine years later Mother Teresa was beatified in St Peter's Square, just a few hundred yards away from the convent chapel. By coincidence, the date of the beatification was also 19 October.

24

A Gift, a Blessing

Standing there that day in St Peter's Square together with thousands of other people – among them groups of poor and handicapped people accompanied by the sisters – I had time to reflect back on some of the different encounters I'd had with Mother Teresa over the years. Many other people – priests among them, but especially, of course, the sisters themselves – had known Mother Teresa far better than I myself. But I was overwhelmed, all the same, by the thought of the privilege of grace I had enjoyed during those years – a grace, a blessing, far beyond anything I had ever deserved or expected.

A few moments after the beatification ceremony was completed, a banner showing Mother Teresa's image was unrolled from the central balcony just over the main door of St Peter's. The particular image chosen was obviously based on one of the hundreds of photographs which had been taken of Mother during her life. And it was a splendid image, truly radiant. When I saw it, I was immediately struck by the ecstasy of joy which illumined Mother's expression. I think I must have gasped, and I'm sure others did as well who were standing near me in the Piazza. Later, at some point before Mass ended, I remember beginning to turn over in my mind the question: what, finally, was revealed in Blessed Teresa of Calcutta? What was the nature of the radiance which shone through her life and work? And I thought: Well, if there is one word which can answer this question, it is the word 'love'. But, then, there came into my mind at once another word, an unexpected word, the word 'emptiness'.

What I mean by 'emptiness' is that Mother Teresa was so free of the weight of self that, when you met her, you almost had the feeling that she was coming towards you – *not* because she was so full and you were so empty, but because, in that moment for her, you were the one person in the world she most wanted to meet. You were her son or her daughter or her brother. And you were also Christ, her *hidden* brother. And she was coming towards you, as if to lean on you, for a moment, or as if somehow she might find rest in your presence. In all my life, I think, I never met anyone with such a radiant lightness of being as Teresa of Calcutta. In her every gesture, there was revealed not simply her own great goodness and strength of character but also something of the unimaginable kindness and goodness of God. In the end it was, I believe, this shining within her – and shining *through* her – of the utter humility and beauty of God which was her greatest gift to those who were fortunate enough to have come to know her, however briefly. I make this point here because, with regard to such illumined or shining knowledge, all of us are among the needy and the beggars, all of us are the poorest of the poor.

Over the years, there were many things Mother Teresa said which I found memorable, things I saw quoted in books and articles, and things I heard from her own lips. But standing there, that day, in the brilliant sunlight of St Peter's Square, there was one small phrase more than any other, which I remembered out of the past, one plain but wondrous statement which sang into my heart: 'Father Paul, God is *love!*'

Remember that the passion of Christ
ends always in the joy of the Resurrection,
so when you feel in your own heart
the suffering of Christ,
remember the Resurrection has to come,
the joy of Easter has to dawn.
Never let anything so fill you with sorrow
as to make you forget
the joy of the Risen Christ!

Teresa of Calcutta

NOTES

2: The Radiance, the Darkness

1. Mother Teresa to Father Josef Neuner, SJ, 6 March 1962. See *Come Be My Light: The Private Writings of the Saint of Calcutta,* edited with commentary by Brian Kolodiejchuk, MC (New York: 2007), pp. 337–8.

3: 'God Wants to Use Nothing'

1. Mother Teresa to Archbishop Périer, SJ, 3 December 1947; *Private Writings,* p. 98. In this letter Mother Teresa refers back to certain remarkable experiences of grace that took place in the previous year.
2. Ibid., p. 96.
3. Ibid., p. 96.
4. Ibid., p. 98.
5. Ibid., p. 98. This further communication was received by Mother Teresa in 1947.
6. With characteristic humility and directness, on 4 April 1955, she admitted to one of her failings in a letter to Archbishop Périer. 'This year,' she wrote, 'I have often been impatient & even sometimes harsh in my remarks – & I have noticed each time I have done the Sisters less good – I always got more from them when I am kind.'

See *Private Writings*, p. 160. In all the meetings I had with Mother Teresa, in Rome and Calcutta, I have to say I witnessed no fault or flaw in her of any kind. That does not mean, however, that she was always perfect. As St Teresa of Avila remarked once in a letter to a friend, 'we never quite become saints in this life'. See Letter to P. Jerónimo Gracián, 31 October 1576, *The Letters of Saint Teresa of Avila*, vol. 1, ed. E. Allison Peers (London: 1980), p. 322.

7. The meditation takes the form of a response by Mother Teresa to the question asked by Jesus in Matthew 16:15: 'Who do you say that I am?' See *Private Writings*, p. 304.

4: A Meeting in Rome

1. See '*Il Testamento di S. Bernadette*', *Rivista di ascetica e mistica* (April/June 1984), pp. 139–40. It was in this *Rivista* or Journal I first came upon the *Testament*. It was presented as a work of Bernadette herself. At a later date, however, I was able to track down the text to its original source. It first appeared in '*Fonte Vive*', vol. VI (September 1960), pp. 304–8. There the *Testament* was given the title '*Il Poema dell'Umiltà*' ('The Poem of Humility'). Fr Pierluigi Torresin, CP was the author and editor of the text. He had put together a number of sayings based on the few small writings of St Bernadette and on her life.
2. By an unusual coincidence, one of Mother Teresa's early spiritual directors had actually encouraged her to look to the example of Bernadette of Lourdes. The 'little Bernadette', he called her, and he noted how Bernadette

had clung to God right to the very end of her life in spite of the demanding trials of 'loneliness, of abandonment, of not being wanted, of darkness of the soul'. See Archbishop Périer to Mother Teresa, July 29 1956; *Private Writings,* pp. 167–8.

3. Mother Teresa to Archbishop Périer, 30 March 1947; *Private Writings,* p. 66.
4. A statement made by Mother Teresa to Father Michael van der Peet; cited in *Private Writings,* p. 294.
5. See '*Il Testamento di S. Bernadette*', *Rivista di ascetica e mistica* (April/June 1984,) p. 140.
6. Mother Teresa to Archbishop Périer, 12 September 1957; *Private Writings,* p. 173.
7. Mother Teresa to Father van der Peet, 26 November 1976; *Private Writings,* p. 278.

5: A Saint of Darkness

1. Mother Teresa to Archbishop Ferdinand Périer, 28 February 1957; *Private Writings,* p. 169.
2. Mother Teresa to Bishop Lawrence Picachy, SJ, 21 September 1962; *Private Writings,* p. 238.
3. Mother Teresa to Bishop Picachy, 9 January 1964; *Private Writings,* p. 245.
4. Mother Teresa to Father Neuner, 17 May 1964; *Private Writings,* p. 248.

6: The Meaning of the Dark Night

1. St John of the Cross, *The Ascent of Mount Carmel,* bk 2, ch. 19, 10, trans. K. Kavanaugh and O. Rodriguez (Washington: 1973), p. 167.

2. Mother Teresa to Father Neuner, 27 November 1969; *Private Writings,* p. 265.
3. St John of the Cross, *The Dark Night,* bk 2, ch. 5, 1, trans, K. Kavanaugh and O. Rodriquez (Washington: 1973), p. 335.
4. Ibid., bk 2, ch. 7, 3, p. 341.
5. Ibid., bk 2, ch. 5, 6, p. 337.
6. Ibid., p. 336.
7. Prayer of Mother Teresa (undated). It was included in a letter sent to Bishop Picachy, 3 July 1959. See *Private Writings,* pp. 186–7. For comparable statements of bewilderment made by other contemplatives undergoing the trial of the dark night, see Appendix VI in *Stages in Prayer* by J. G. Arintero, OP, trans. K. Pond (London: 1957), pp. 161–7.
8. *The Dark Night,* bk I, ch. 10, 1, p. 316.
9. Ibid., bk 2, ch. 6, 2, p. 338.
10. Extract from a prayer composed by Mother Teresa, and sent to Bishop Picachy on 3 September 1959. See *Private Writings,* pp. 192–3.
11. See *The Dark Night,* bk I, ch. 9, 2, p. 313.
12. Ibid., bk I, ch. 9, 3, p. 313. St John is not, of course, unaware that a certain 'melancholia' can, on occasion, accompany even the most authentic experience of 'the dark night'. See *The Dark Night,* bk I, ch. 9, 3, p. 314.

7: Varieties of the Dark Night

1. See *The Dark Night,* bk I, ch 9, 1–9, pp. 313–16.
2. Ibid., bk I, ch 9, 8, p. 315.
3. Ibid., bk I, ch 9, 6, p. 315.

4. John Paul II, *Master in the Faith: Apostolic Letter on the Occasion of the Fourth Centenary of the Death of Saint John of the Cross*, III, 14; reproduced in *Catholic International*, vol. 2, 5 (March 1991), p. 207.
5. Ibid., III, 14, p. 207. John Paul does not hesitate to refer, at one point, to 'the dark night of the war'. See 'Introduction', p. 203.
6. Ibid., III, 14, p. 207.

8: The Feelings of an Unbeliever

1. *The Ascent of Mount Carmel*, bk 2, ch. 6, 2, trans. K. Kavanaugh and O. Rodriquez (Washington: 1973), p. 119.
2. According to Josef Pieper this 'mental unrest' is 'an inescapable accompaniment of the act of belief'. Pieper bases his judgment on the teaching of St Thomas Aquinas. 'It is astonishing,' he writes, 'to see with what outspoken candour a theologian such as Thomas Aquinas describes this element of uncertainty in the act of belief.' See Josef Pieper, *Faith, Hope, Love,* trans. R. and C. Winston (San Francisco: 1997), pp. 52–3.
3. Letter to a non-monastic friend, 16 January 1923 in *The Spiritual Letters of Dom John Chapman, OSB.*, ed. R. Hudleston (London: 1935), p. 47; cited in Carol Zaleski, 'The Dark Night of Mother Teresa,' *First Things*, 133 (May 2003), p. 26.
4. This extraordinary statement can be found in Tauler's *Sermon for the Fifth Sunday after Trinity.* See Oliver Davies: *God Within: The Mystical Tradition of Northern Europe* (London: 1988), pp. 88–9.

9: 'Where Is Jesus?'

1. Mother Teresa to Archbishop Périer, 28 February 1957; *Private Writings,* pp. 169–70.
2. Mother Teresa to Bishop Picachy, 6 November 1958; *Private Writings,* p. 180.
3. St John of the Cross, *The Spiritual Canticle,* stanza 17, I, trans. K. Kavanaugh and O. Rodriquez (Washington: 1973), p. 479.
4. Ibid., p. 478.
5. For the description of this incident I am indebted to a written testimony sent to me by Bishop William Curlin on 10 December 2006.
6. The details in this account were described to me by Bishop Curlin during a phone conversation on 18 June 2006.
7. Mother Teresa to Bishop Picachy, 21 September 1962; *Private Writings,* p. 238.
8. Letter of Father Neuner to the present author, 10 March 2006.

10: Absence and Presence

1. Bishop Curlin repeated these words of Mother Teresa to the author in a phone conversation on 18 June 2006.
2. Mother Teresa to Archbishop Périer, 7 November 1958; *Private Writings,* p. 177.
3. Extract of Mother Teresa's speech, Berlin, 8 June 1980. See Appendix A in Eileen Egan, *Such a Vision of the Street: Mother Teresa, The Spirit and the Work* (New York: 1985), p. 427.

4. Mother Teresa to Father Michael van der Peet, 19 June 1976; *Private Writings*, p. 274.
5. See *The Dark Night*, bk I, ch. 9, 3, pp. 313.

11: Christian Faith and the Dark Night

1. Cardinal Ratzinger's statement occurs in a document issued by the Congregation for the Doctrine of the Faith on 15 October 1989. See *Letter to the Bishops of the Catholic Church on Some Aspects of Christian Meditation* (*Orationis Formas*) no. 24, footnote 28.
2. Ibid., no. 24. This statement does not exclude, I think, the possibility that 'certain mystical graces' given to the founder or, in this case, to the foundress, might also be given by God to others in the same institute. What is excluded, however, is the idea that, in a particular institute, members should seek, as if by right – in virtue of their religious vocation – to have a share in the founder's 'personal charism of prayer'.
3. *The Cloud of Unknowing*, ed. W. Johnston (New York: 1973), pp. 48–9.
4. See *A Message from Contemplative Monks to the Synod of Bishops on the Possibility of Man's Entering into Dialogue with the Ineffable God*, pp. 4–5. The 'Message' was first published as a tiny pamphlet in 1967. (No place of publication is indicated.)
5. Ibid., pp. 5–6.

12: Paradox or Contradiction?

1. Mother Teresa to Bishop Picachy, 21 September 1962; *Private Writings*, p. 238.

2. Statement of Mother Teresa quoted in a testimony of Fr Albert Huart, SJ. See *Private Writings,* p. 306.
3. Mother Teresa to Father Neuner, datable to 8 November 1961; *Private Writings,* p. 226.
4. Mother Teresa to Father Neuner, undated but written probably during the retreat of April 1961; *Private Writings,* p. 210.
5. Prayer of Mother Teresa enclosed in a letter to Bishop Picachy, 3 September 1959; *Private Writings,* p. 193.
6. Pope Paul VI, General Audience, 26 June 1974. See 'Suffering in the Christian Life', in *Pope Paul and the Spirit,* ed. E. D. O'Connor (Indiana: 1978), p. 209. A similar teaching was given to the medieval Dominican mystic, St Catherine of Siena. At one point in her famous 'Dialogue' with God the Father, Catherine is told that the soul of the good Christian can, at one and the same time, be both 'blissful and afflicted'. See *Il Dialogo della divina provvidenza,* no. 78, ed. G. Cavallini (Rome: 1968), pp. 178–9.
7. Ibid., p. 208.
8. Ibid., p. 209.
9. Mother Teresa to Bishop Picachy, 8 January 1964; *Private Writings,* p. 245.
10. Mother Teresa to Bishop Picachy, 26 December 1959; *Private Writings,* p. 198.

13: The Sunshine of Darkness

1. Mother Teresa to Father Neuner, most probably 11 April 1961; *Private Writings,* p. 214.
2. Words of Mother Teresa, cited in a written testimony

sent by Bishop Curlin to the author on 10 December, 2006.

3. Mother Teresa to Father Neuner, undated, most probably written during the retreat of April 1961; *Private Writings*, p. 212.
4. Mother Teresa to Father Neuner, 12 May 1962; *Private Writings*, p. 232.
5. Mother Teresa to Bishop Picachy, 7 August 1960; *Private Writings*, p. 200.
6. Mother Teresa to Archbishop Périer, 30 March 1947; *Private Writings*, p. 170. Mother Teresa could, on occasion, be somewhat hypersensitive. Once, to a correspondent who failed to send her good wishes for her feast-day, she wrote: 'I missed your letter for my feast. In 20 years this is the first time.' Letter to Archbishop Périer, 4 October 1956; *Private Writings*, p. 377.
7. A phrase used by Mother Teresa in a written explanation of the original Constitutions of the MC Sisters (undated); *Private Writings*, p. 141.
8. Mother Teresa to Archbishop Périer, 21 June 1950; *Private Writings*, p. 168.

15: Mother Teresa at Mass

1. Cited in Raghu Rai and Navin Chawla, *Faith and Compassion: The Life and Work of Mother Teresa* (Shaftesbury: 1996), p. 50.
2. Ibid., p. 93.

16: A Mission to Love

1. Letter of Mother Teresa to Malcolm Muggeridge; cited

in Muggeridge, *Conversion: A Spiritual Journey* (London: 1989), pp. 138–9. See also *Private Writings,* p. 280.

17: Mother Teresa and the Small Thérèse

1. Thérèse to Celine, Letter CXXIV, Carmel, 2 August 1893. See *Collected Letters of Saint Thérèse of Lisieux*, vol. 2, trans. F. J. Sheed (London: 1972), p. 172.
2. Ibid., p. 173.
3. Ibid., p. 172.
4. The Washington talk was published later under the title, 'Whatever you did unto one of the least you did unto me.' See *Communio* 21 (Spring 1994), p. 145.

18: The Demands of Love

1. Extract of Mother Teresa's speech, National Prayer Breakfast, Washington, DC, 3 February 1994. See 'Whatever you did unto one of the least, you did it to me,' *Communio* 21 (Spring 1994), p. 150. See also *Private Writings,* p. 281.
2. Journal of Mother Teresa, 16 February 1949 (hereafter Journal). See *Private Writings,* p. 133. The keeping of this record was requested by Archbishop Périer. Begun towards the end of 1948, it was concluded on 11 June 1949.
3. Ibid., *Private Writings,* p. 134.
4. Journal, 28 February 1949; *Private Writings,* p. 134.
5. Mother Teresa to Archbishop Périer, 18 March 1953; *Private Writings,* p. 149.
6. Mother Teresa's letter to Sister Mary of the Trinity, from which this extract is taken, belongs to the archives

of a Dominican contemplative convent in the United States. Since this is the first time these particular words (and others later) of Mother Teresa, have found their way into print, I am happy here to express my gratitude to the Prioress and community of the Convent of Our Lady of Grace, North Guilford.

19: A Grace of Surrender

1. Hans Urs von Balthasar, 'Beyond Action and Contemplation', in *Explorations in Theology IV: Spirit and Institution,* trans. E. T. Oaks (San Francisco: 1995) p. 304.
2. Ibid., p. 306.
3. Ibid., pp. 305–6. The astonishing 'readiness' of Mother Teresa to be consumed for the salvation of the world was made evident in April 1942 when she took a private vow never to refuse God anything.
4. John of the Cross explains that, as a direct result of the inflow of God into the soul during the dark night, the soul acquires such a profound humility 'it considers itself to be nothing'. This humility is the beauty of holiness itself. But the soul, conscious only of its own 'dryness and wretchedness', judges that 'others are better'. See *The Dark Night,* bk I, ch. 12, 2 and 7, p. 321 and p. 323.
5. As a gloss here on Mother Teresa's profound sense of being 'exposed to the whole world', the following passage from the French mystic, Simone Weil, is worth noting. Weil writes: 'To be innocent is to bear the weight of the entire universe. It is to throw away the counterweight. In emptying ourselves we expose our-

selves to all the pressure of the surrounding universe.' See *Gravity and Grace,* trans. E. Craufurd (London: 1972) p. 83.

20: Profound Vision, Simple Words

1. See *The Sayings of the Desert Fathers,* no. 7, ed. and trans. B. Ward (Kalamazoo: 1984), p. 103.
2. Just before she began her work for the poorest of the poor in Calcutta Mother Teresa, in a letter to Archbishop Périer dated 13 January 1947, spoke of her willingness to be utterly consumed – 'to burn myself completely' – in order that Christ might become better known and loved. See *Private Writings,* p. 52.

22: A Spirit of Freedom and Joy

1. Mother Teresa to Sister Rose Thérèse [later Sister Mary of the Holy Trinity], 14 March 1966. (Letter in the archives of the Dominican Contemplative Convent, North Guilford, USA.)
2. Ibid., 10 February 1967. 'It is in her letters,' observed Malcolm Muggeridge, 'that the laughter which, with Mother Teresa, is never far away comes over most clearly – those letters, so wonderfully beautiful and wonderfully funny, that she writes late at night, or in trains and airplanes, always in her own hand and on the cheapest possible notepaper.' See *Mother Teresa of Calcutta: A Gift for God* (New York: 1975), pp. 5–6.
3. Extract of Mother Teresa's speech, Institute on Religious Life, Chicago, Illinois, 14 June 1981. The talk was later published under the title 'Young People Want

to see our Undivided Love for Christ.' See *Religious Life,* vol. 5, 6 (July/August 1981), pp. 6–7.

23: On Earth and in Heaven

1. Mother Teresa to Father Neuner, 6 March 1962; *Private Writings,* pp. 337–8.

ABOUT PARACLETE PRESS

Who We Are

Paraclete Press is an ecumenical publisher of books and recordings on Christian spirituality. our publishing represents a full expression of Christian belief and practice—from Catholic to evangelical, from Protestant to orthodox.

Paraclete Press is the publishing arm of the Community of Jesus, an ecumenical monastic community in the Benedictine tradition. As such, we are uniquely positioned in the marketplace without connection to a large corporation and with informal relationships to many branches and denominations of faith.

We like it best when people buy our books from booksellers, our partners in successfully reaching as wide an audience as possible.

What We Are Doing

Books • Paraclete Press publishes books that show the richness and depth of what it means to be Christian. Although Benedictine spirituality is at the heart of all that we do, we publish books that reflect the Christian experience across many cultures, time periods, and houses of worship.

We publish books that nourish the vibrant life of the church and its people—books about spiritual practice, formation, history, ideas, and customs.

We have several different series of books within Paraclete Press, includ ing the best-selling Living Library series of modernized classic texts; A Voice from the Monastery—giving voice to men and women monastics about what it means to live a spiritual life today; award-winning literary faith fiction; and books that explore Judaism and Islam and discover how these faiths inform Christian thought and practice.

Recordings • From Gregorian chant to contemporary American choral works, our music recordings celebrate the richness of sacred choral music through the centuries. Paraclete is proud to distribute the recordings of the internationally acclaimed choir Gloriæ Dei Cantores, who have been praised for their "rapt and fathomless spiritual intensity" by American Record Guide, and the Gloriæ Dei Cantores Schola, which specializes in the study and performance of Gregorian chant. Paraclete is also the exclusive North American distributor of the recordings of the Monastic Choir of St. Peter's Abbey in Solesmes, France, long considered to be a leading authority on Gregorian chant performance.

ALSO AVAILABLE FROM PARACLETE PRESS

Seeking His Mind

M. Basil Pennington, OCSO

$14.95 in trade paper
ISBN: 978-1-55725-562-4

ACCORDING TO BASIL PENNINGTON, one of the spiritual masters of the last half century, those who visited his monastery wanted to know the Christian method of transformation. He replies that it is *lectio divina*—an ancient practice of sacred reading. "If each day a word of the Lord can truly come alive for us and can form our mind and heart, we will have that mind of Christ."

Words of Light

Inspiration from the Letters of Padre Pio
Compiled and with an Introduction by
Fr. Raniero Cantalamessa

$23.95 in hardcover
ISBN: 978-1-55725-569-3

IF YOU ARE INTERESTED IN THE COMPLEXITIES AND CHALLENGES OF CONTEMPORARY FAITH, you will benefit from these short teachings, counsels, and recollections culled from some of Padre Pio's most personal writings.

"[In these letters]I quickly discovered
the same states of soul that were described by the great mystics.
Padre Pio's own 'dark night' was in no way inferior to that
described by John of the Cross; and equally the 'living flame' of
his love for God dazzles the reader and allows them to catch a
glimpse of another world."

—Fr. Raniero Cantalamessa, from the Introduction

Available from most booksellers or through Paraclete Press:
www.paracletepress.com; 1-800-451-5006.
Try your local bookstore first.